The Great Glen Way

Jacquetta Megarry
and
Sandra Bardwell

Rucksack Readers

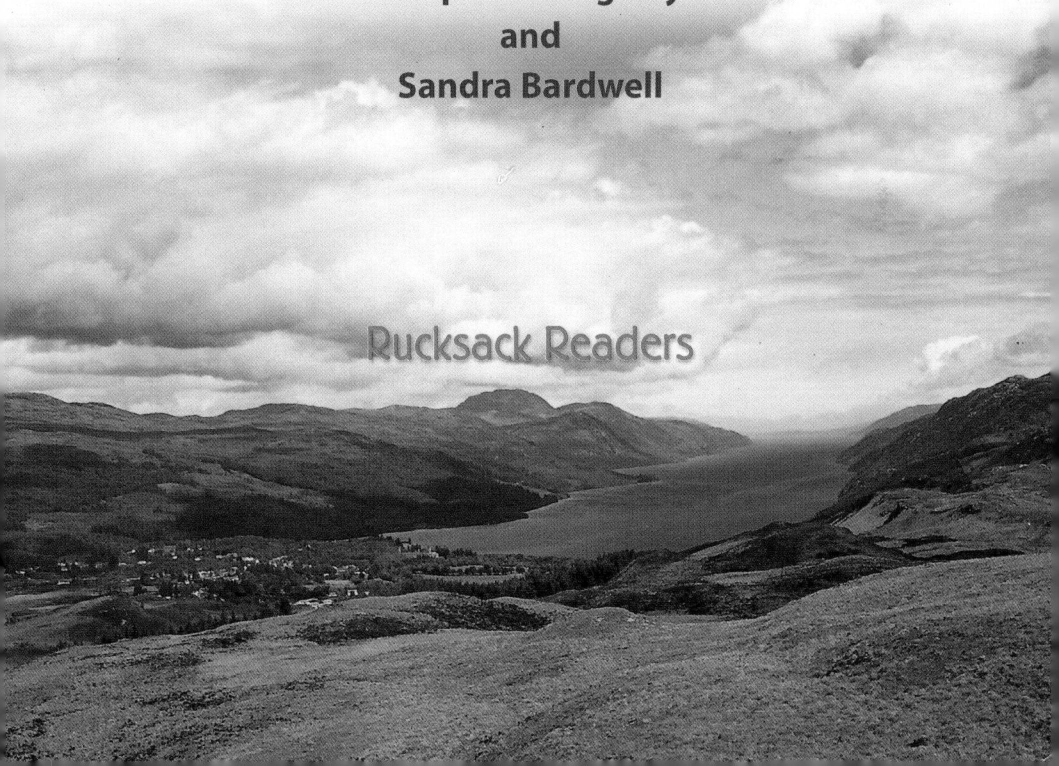

The Great Glen Way: Official Rucksack Reader Guide

Third edition published 2005 by Rucksack Readers, Landrick Lodge, Dunblane, FK15 0HY, UK
Telephone 01786 824 696 (+44 1786 824 696)
Fax 01786 825 090 (+44 1786 825 090)
Email info@rucsacs.com
Website **www.rucsacs.com**

ISBN 1-898481-24-5

British Library cataloguing in publication data: a catalogue record for this book is available from the British Library.

Designed in Scotland by WorkHorse (info@workhorse.co.uk)

Reprographics by HK Scanner Arts International Ltd
Printed in China by Hong Kong Graphics & Printing Ltd

The Fort William town plan is based on mapping by Wendy Price Cartographic Services with information from the Royal Commission on the Ancient and Historical Monuments of Scotland (RCAHMS).

Note on the third edition

The Great Glen Way's continuing popularity has allowed us to create this new edition. We are grateful to readers for their past comments and suggestions which have led to many improvements. Further feedback is always welcome, ideally by email to **info@rucsacs.com**.

Walkers are advised to check with the official website for updates and advice before setting out: **www.greatglenway.com**

Some parts of the Way are exposed and somewhat remote. You are responsible for your own safety, and for ensuring that your clothing, food and equipment are suited to your needs. The publisher cannot accept any liability for any ill-health, accident or loss arising directly or indirectly from reading this book.

The Great Glen Way: contents

Long-distance walks in the Highlands

Long-distance walks run like threads through Scotland's history. Walk one and you're walking in the footsteps of drovers, pilgrims, soldiers, clansmen and cattle-rustlers. The map shows five of Scotland's finest long walks: see page 63 for details of companion guidebooks to the other four.

The Great Glen Way runs 73 miles from Fort William to Inverness. It passes Britain's highest mountain, follows its greatest geological fault along the shores of its most famous loch and finishes at Inverness, Scotland's most northerly city and the capital of the Highlands. Much of it runs alongside the Caledonian Canal, an outstanding feature of Victorian engineering in Scotland.

Most of the walking is straightforward, along canal towpaths and forest tracks, but there are some challenging sections and the final day is 18 miles (29 km) long.

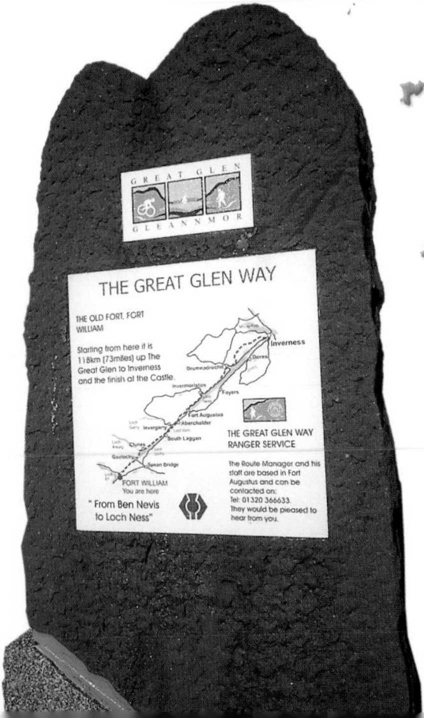

Cateran Trail	64 miles	103 km
Great Glen Way	73 miles	117 km
Rob Roy Way	79 miles	126 km
Speyside Way	84 miles	135 km
West Highland Way	95 miles	153 km

Stone markers in Fort William and Inverness define the start and finish of the Great Glen Way: see also page 58

Planning to walk the Way

The Great Glen Way is a very appealing walk, one that any healthy person of any age can tackle and realistically expect to complete. It is easier than the West Highland Way, for example, being shorter overall, less strenuous and mainly on better terrain. Sensible planning and preparation are still important. Well in advance, you should complete a few long hikes, if only to test your feet and gear. If you lack experience, obtain our 'Notes for novices': see page 61. The route is fully waymarked with the 'thistle in a hexagon' logo: see page 7.

Committed walkers may seize the chance to combine the West Highland and Great Glen Ways, walking from Glasgow to Inverness over two weeks: see page 63 for further reading and contacts. This challenging expedition takes you through 168 miles (270 km) of spectacular scenery and Highland heritage. It could be considered one of the grandest long walks in Britain.

No-one should undertake the Great Glen Way casually, because the weather in Scotland is so unpredictable. On any given day in the Highlands, you may experience weather typical of any season, and perhaps all four. This adds charm and variety to the experience, but also makes it important to have the right clothing and attitude.

This book has been planned in the recommended direction, walking north-east from Fort William to Inverness. The prevailing wind in Scotland is south-westerly, so you are more likely to have the wind at your back. That way, the longest day is your final one into Inverness, by which time you'll be well into your stride. Finally, on average there should be less rain as you move northeast: Inverness has annual rainfall of 25 inches, compared with Fort William's 80. You may find this good for morale.

How long will it take?

Most people spread the walk over five or six days, but some take longer, depending on the time available and the pace they find comfortable. Table 1 shows distances and proposes two options. Don't underestimate the time you need: there is no point in being among some of Scotland's finest scenery and wildlife unless you have time to appreciate it. Read section 2.4 to decide whether you want to build in time for extra hill walks. These could add anything from half a day to a couple of overnights to the overall duration.

Table 1 Possible overnight stops for a six- or five-day walk

	Six-day		Five-day	
	miles	*km*	*miles*	*km*
Fort William				
	10	16	10	16
Gairlochy				
	13	21	13	21
South Laggan				
	10	16		
Fort Augustus			18	29
	8	13		
Invermoriston				
	14	22	14	22
Drumnadrochit				
	18	29	18	29
Inverness				
Total distance	73	117	73	117

Plan how you will reach the start and return from the finish points. Depending on where you're coming from, you may need to overnight in Fort William and/or Inverness. Table 2 gives estimated times by various travel methods, and there are suggestions for combining the Way with activities other than walking on page 8. If you live near the Great Glen, you could instead walk the Way in sections, for example over three week-ends, taking advantage of the regular bus services along the A82: see page 62.

Although Part 3 describes the Way in five sections that correspond roughly with the five map panels, you might well spend longer. Fort Augustus is the natural half-way point, and a great place to overnight: see page 47. On the five-day option you wouldn't stay there at all. Note that the last day is long. Lack of accommodation makes it difficult for an unsupported walker to spread this over two days, unless camping at Wester Laide. Some tour operators offer to split the section at Blackfold, using vehicle transfers to shuttle between Blackfold and Drumnadrochit.

Wherever you choose to make overnight stops, don't leave accommodation to chance. It can be scarce both out of season and in high summer, and booking is essential. Specialist tour operators can organise it all for you, or you can research the options by contacting Tourist Information Centres and searching the web: see the official website **www.greatglenway.com** and/or request the free booklet *Accommodation & Services Guide*: see pages 61–62.

Planning your travel

To plan your travel, consult the cover maps together with Table 2 below. There are good train and coach services to Fort William via Glasgow and Edinburgh, and also good return connections from Inverness back to Glasgow and Edinburgh.

Table 2 shows the fastest scheduled times for bus and train as of 2005. Car journey times are the fastest likely within speed limits, with no allowance for traffic hold-ups and minimal fuel/meal stops. All figures are rough guidelines only. Check schedules in advance, as winter timetables may be restricted: see page 62 for contact details.

Table 2 Distances and journey times between selected places

	Approx miles	*km*	*by bus*	*by train*	*by car*
Glasgow / Fort William	100	160	3h	3h 45m	2h 30m
Edinburgh / Fort William	145	235	4h	5h	3h 30m
Inverness / Fort William	70	110	2h	n/a	1h 30m
Inverness / Glasgow	165	265	4h	3h 30m	3h 30m
Inverness / Edinburgh	160	265	3h 30m	3h 30m	3h 30m
Glasgow / Edinburgh	45	70	1h	50m	45m

Inverness Airport is 10 miles east of the city and has direct flights to Edinburgh, Glasgow, several regional airports and to London. In 2005 these included Heathrow (bmi), Gatwick (British Airways and easyJet) and Luton (easyJet). Budget fares are available on most flights subject to the usual restrictions. See page 62 for contact details for airlines, buses and trains.

If you are walking alone, public transport will simplify the return to your starting-point. If you are in a group with a non-walking driver, he or she can easily arrange to rendezvous with hikers, because the A82 trunk road runs up the Great Glen. The drop-down map (back cover) shows bus stops, railway stations and main roads in more detail.

What is the best time of year?

Fortunately for those who have little choice over their holiday dates, there is no bad time of year to walk the Way. Be prepared for cold, wet and windy weather at any time of year and you could be pleasantly surprised. You may be lucky enough, even in winter, to experience sunshine and clear air.

Here are a few factors to think about:

- Winter is less flexible for walkers, because the days are so much shorter: high latitude means that the hours of daylight vary from 6-7 hours in late December to 17-18 in late June.
- Winter restricts your choice of side-trips, which may be open only from April to October.
- From May to September, expect pests such as midges (small biting insects) and/or clegs (horse-flies), especially in still weather.
- On winter timetables, public transport is less frequent.
- In summer, many more tourists are around and there's heavy pressure on accommodation; however, in winter many B&Bs are closed for the season.

On balance, and if you are free to choose, the ideal months are probably May/ June and September/early October. July and August are the busiest times for visitors, so demand for accommodation may be heavy.

Combining the Way with other activities

The Great Glen area offers scope for many other activities. If you have two weeks to spare and like messing around with boats, you could hire a boat to sail one-way (sail or motor) and return on foot (or vice versa). There is ample scope for combining walking with golf, fishing, genealogy or leisure and many great Highland hotels. Contact details are given on pages 61-2.

If you are on holiday with reluctant walkers or non-walkers, remember that the A82 is well served by buses (around six a day). Stops are marked on the drop-down map, and people can join or leave your walking group along the way.

The Great Glen Cycle Route, also known as the Great Glen Mountain Bike Trail, shares various sections of the Way. On shared sections, walkers and cyclists need to be aware of each other, and cyclists should cycle responsibly, giving way to walkers on narrow paths. You might also meet horseriders in places.

There is plenty of scope for climbing hills and mountains: see pages 26-31. Depending on the season, this could add to the amount of clothing and gear that you need to bring.

The Scottish Outdoor Access Code

The Scottish Outdoor Access Code interprets the access rights established by law. It took effect in February 2005: see panel below. The Great Glen Way attracts large numbers of visitors, some of whom may lack experience of livestock and other countryside issues. Be aware that the countryside provides a livelihood for its residents and show consideration for them and their livestock. Lambing can occur any time from March to June: never disturb pregnant ewes, nor approach young lambs. Cattle can be fiercely protective of their young, and walkers should give them a wide berth, especially if there are calves around.

Know the Code before you go . . . Enjoy Scotland's outdoors - responsibly

Everyone has the right to be on most land and inland water providing they act responsibly.
Your access rights and responsibilities are explained fully in the Scottish Outdoor Access Code.

Whether you're in the outdoors or managing the outdoors, the key things are to

- take responsibility for your own actions
- respect the interests of other people
- care for the environment.

Find out more by visiting **www.outdooraccess-scotland.com** or phoning your local Scottish Natural Heritage office.

SCOTTISH
OUTDOOR ACCESS CODE

Dogs

Walkers must keep their dog(s) under proper control. Before deciding to take your dog along the Way, remember that many accommodations do not accept dogs: check carefully before booking.

Your main responsibilities when walking a dog in the countryside are:

- never let your dog worry or attack livestock
- don't take your dog into fields where there are lambs, calves or other young animals
- if you go into a field of farm animals, keep your dog(s) on a short lead or under close control and keep as far as possible from the animals
- if cattle react aggressively and move towards you, keep calm, let the dog go and take the shortest, safest route out of the field
- during the bird breeding season (usually April to July), keep your dog under close control or on a short lead in open country and near water
- if your dog defecates in a public open place, pick up and remove its mess.

Camping and low-cost accommodation

Commercial campsites generally have toilets and showers; some have laundries. You'll find them along the Way near Fort William (Glen Nevis), at Gairlochy, Fort Augustus, Invermoriston, Drumnadrochit, Wester Laide (near Abriachan) and near Inverness. Details are on the official website and in the leaflet.

Wild camping means low-impact independent camping without facilities. It's allowed for small numbers for up to two or three nights in any one place. Avoid camping in enclosed fields of crops or farm animals, and keep well away from buildings, roads or historic structures. Take extra care to avoid disturbing deer stalking or grouse shooting. If you wish to camp close to a house or building, seek the owner's permission. Be careful to leave no traces of your campsite.

There are youth hostels along the Way at Fort William (Glen Nevis), Loch Lochy, Loch Ness (Alltsigh) and Inverness. Walkers of any age can stay at these, and joining SYHA, the organisation that runs them, is optional. There are also independent hostels at Fort William, Spean Bridge, Invergarry, Fort Augustus, Drumnadrochit and Inverness: see page 62 for contact details for SYHA and for Scottish Independent Hostels.

What to bring

People vary widely in what they need for comfort and whether they expect to carry everything for themselves or to rely on a baggage handling service. Choice of accommodation also affects whether you need to pack a towel or sleeping bag liner, for example. If you are camping, offloading the heavy stuff to a baggage handler may let you enjoy your walk more. If you are staying in B&Bs or hostels, start by reviewing what you need to walk comfortably each day. If the overnight extras are little more than clean underwear and a toothbrush, you may decide to carry them so as to remain independent.

Baggage handling in the Great Glen is offered by several firms, and you can deal with them directly, or, if using a tour operator to organise your accommodation, this service is often included. Details are given in the *Accommodation & Services Guide* booklet (updated annually) and on the website: see page 61.

Think carefully about what to take and do any specialised shopping ahead of time. Once on the Way, shops are scarce. There is no shop or bank between Fort William and Fort Augustus – although one shop is a short detour from Laggan Bridge. Likewise, between Drumnadrochit and Inverness there is no shop, pub or tearoom, so make sure you have enough food and drink to last all day.

Packing checklist

The checklist below refers to your daytime needs, and is divided into essential and desirable. Experienced walkers may disagree about what belongs in each category, but novices may appreciate a starting-point. Normally you will be wearing the first three or four items and carrying the rest in your rucksack.

Essential

- comfortable, waterproof walking boots
- specialist walking socks
- breathable clothing in layers
- waterproof jacket and over-trousers
- hat and gloves
- water carrier and plenty of water (or purification tablets/drops)
- enough food to last between supply points
- guidebook and/or maps
- first aid kit including blister treatment
- toiletries and overnight necessities
- insect repellent and sun protection (May to September)
- rucksack (at least 35 litres)
- waterproof rucksack cover or liner, e.g. bin (garbage) bag
- enough cash in pounds sterling.

Credit cards are not always acceptable and cash machines are sparse along the Way. Bin bags have many uses e.g. store wet clothing or prevent hypothermia (cut holes for your head and arms).

Desirable

- compass, map, whistle and torch: essential if you are doing any hill climbing or hiking in winter
- walking pole(s)
- binoculars: useful for navigation and spotting wildlife
- camera (ideally light and rugged), also spare batteries, film or memory
- pouch or secure pockets, to keep small items handy but safe
- gaiters (to keep mud and water off trouser legs and boots)
- toilet tissue (biodegradable)
- water purification tablets or drops
- spare socks: changing socks at lunchtime can relieve damp feet
- spare shoes (e.g. trainers or trekking sandals)
- spare bootlaces
- small towel
- notebook and pen.

Camping

If you are camping, you need more gear, including tent, groundsheet, sleeping mat and a warm sleeping bag. You may also want a camping stove, fuel, cooking utensils and food. Your rucksack will have to be much larger and heavier, with a capacity of about 50-80 litres. Camping could add about 10 kg to the weight of your rucksack: previous experience is advisable.

Two final issues: first, where should you 'go' if caught short on the Way? The official advice is

- Use public toilets where available: Fort William, Corpach, Fort Augustus, Invermoriston, Drumnadrochit, Abriachan and Inverness. Also, some canal-side toilets are available for use by walkers: ask the lock-keeper, who also holds the key.
- If a toilet is not available, choose a discreet spot at least 50 yards away from paths and buildings, preferably further, and as far as possible from any water course. Please bury waste in a deep hole; some people carry a trowel for digging, others improvise with boot or poles.

Locks and bridges are staffed by helpful keepers (Tomnahurich Bridge)

Second: what about mobile phones? Never rely on one for personal safety: reception may be poor or non-existent, so even if the battery is well charged you can't be sure of getting through. If you carry one anyway, please consider others when using it. Mobile chatter can interrupt the peace of the countryside and may disturb wildlife.

2·1 Loch Ness and the Great Glen fault

Loch Ness extends over one third of the Great Glen's length and dominates the northern half of the Way, stretching from Fort Augustus to a few miles short of Inverness. It's about 10,000 years old, dating from the end of the last Ice Age when the Great Glen was occupied by a massive glacier. Loch Ness is the centre of an area of outstanding natural beauty, with significant wildlife interest in its waters, around its shores and in its secret side glens. This section covers first the loch and its famous wildlife, then the formation of the Great Glen.

With an average depth of over 600 feet and a length of 23 miles, Loch Ness holds over two cubic miles of water – more than all the lakes and reservoirs in England and Wales put together, and three times as much as Loch Lomond. Draining water from a huge area (700 square miles), it forms one of the largest freshwater systems in Europe. At its deepest point near Urquhart Castle, soundings have recorded over 750 feet (225 m), so it's deeper even than the North Sea. However, the rock bed is covered in thick sediment and clay, so its true depth is greater than has yet been recorded.

Loch Ness is Britain's greatest freshwater system

Because of its great depth, Loch Ness has never been known to freeze. It is so massive that it affects the surrounding land, where snow seldom lies for very long. Most of its waters never become colder than 5° C, even after prolonged sub-zero weather. During the summer months, layers of warmer water lie above the denser colder mass, with a region of sharp temperature change called a thermocline. The water is still too cold for many living things, and some of its inhabitants are left over from glacial times. The combination of steep contours, wind and waves makes its shores inhospitable.

What lives in Loch Ness?

It is Scotland's most famous loch mainly because of persistent reports of sightings of a monster generally known as 'Nessie'. Although Loch Morar is even deeper, plumbing depths of over 1000 feet, its alleged monster Morag has never rivalled Nessie's worldwide fame.

The monster legend dates from 565 AD when St Columba is said to have banished a creature from Loch Ness's northern end. Published reports date from 1868, when the *Inverness Courier* first mentioned the 'tradition of a huge fish gambolling in the loch'. Headlines were made by the 1933 sightings during major works on the A82, when the *Courier* again reported 'a strange spectacle on Loch Ness'.

In 1934 the the monster industry gained impetus from the publication of surgeon R K Wilson's photograph of a serpentine neck rising from a humped body. This infamous hoax was followed by hundreds of fresh photographs and thousands of sightings. Many sincere and frightened eye-witnesses described strange creatures of various shapes and sizes. Various causes have been put forward for these sightings, for example mirages and atmospheric illusions, drifting logs, boat wakes, diving birds, swimming deer, visiting seals, otter's tails and huge migrant fish.

In the 1960s the Loch Ness Investigation Bureau made systematic searches, first on the surface, then underwater, using mini-submarines and sonar. In 1987 Operation Deepscan had 20 motor cruisers sweeping the entire loch with a sonar curtain. Later, the Rosetta Project brought back long columns of sediment collected from the floor; these time capsules show how pollution and radioactivity have plumbed the depths. The scientific data collected by these investigations is stranger than the monster fiction; it is presented imaginatively by the Loch Ness 2000 experience (see page 52).

Food chain in the open water of Loch Ness

Loch Ness is relatively poor in nutrients compared with, for example, Loch Lomond. Although there are occasional migrant seals in pursuit of salmon, the top resident predator in the Loch Ness food chain is the Ferox trout. It is the large fish shown above in pursuit of a shoal of five Arctic charr, its main food source. Charr have been netted from as deep as 730 feet, the deepest recorded fish catch to date. They are relicts of the Ice Age.

Arctic charr in turn feed directly on plankton - tiny organisms that are vital to the food chain. The creatures shown above at lower centre and right are animal plankton, less than a millimetre long (*Bythotrephes* and *Diaptomus*). Animal plankton feed on even smaller plant plankton such as those shown at top right (*Tabellaria*) and bottom left (*Asterionella*). Based on analysis of the food chain, scientists have calculated that there simply isn't enough food in the loch to sustain a resident population of very large predators.

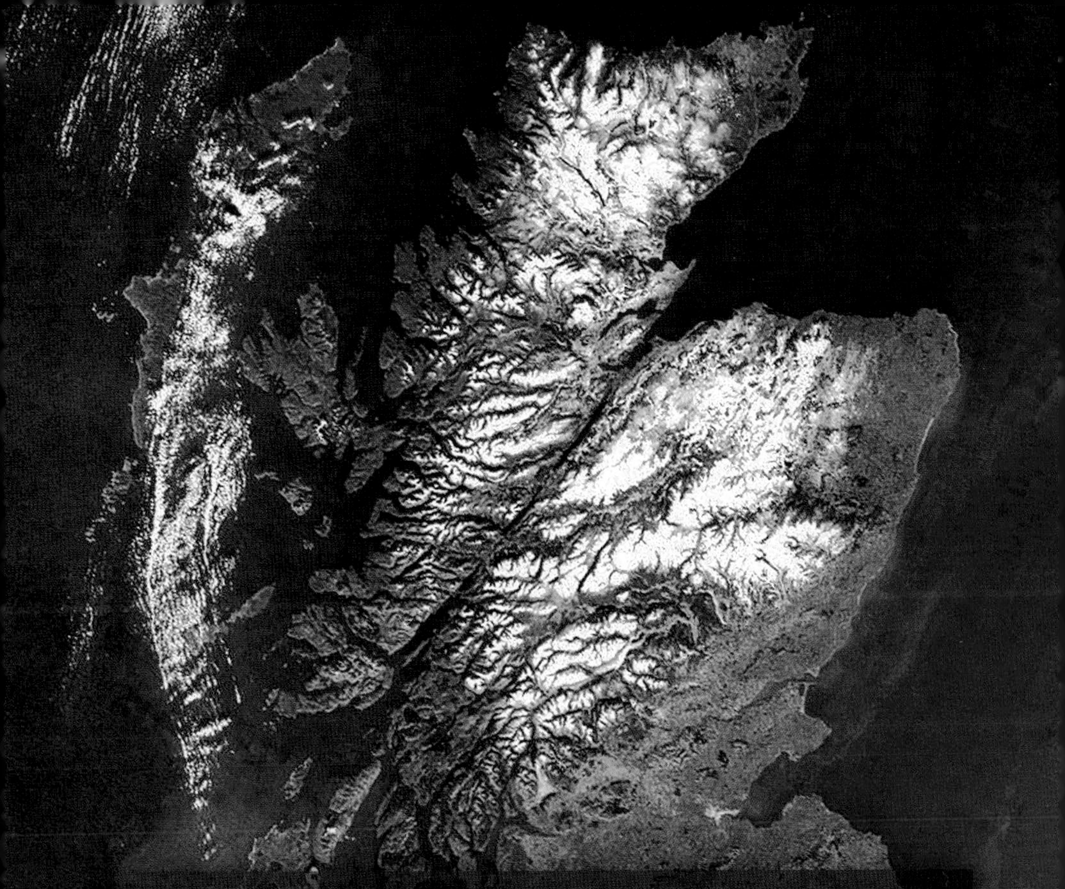

The Great Glen fault

This glen is Scotland's longest, and is known by three names: the Great Glen, Glen Mor (the Gaelic equivalent) or Glen Albyn. It is unusual in that it leads to open water at both ends, to Loch Linnhe and the Moray Firth. In effect, it joins the Atlantic Ocean to the North Sea, almost making an island of north-west Scotland.

The glen follows the line of a major geological fault created about 380 million years ago. North-west Scotland was originally joined to parts of Canada, Greenland and northern Norway. Geologists agree that there was a major upheaval about that time, although theories differ about the fault's exact formation. According to W Q Kennedy, the whole land mass sheared off and was shifted 65 miles to the south-west.

In the Ice Age about 20,000 years ago, giant glaciers covered nearly all of Scotland and northern England. The ice was up to a mile thick in places, wiping out plant and animal life, and scouring a wide corridor along the line of the fault. This is still Britain's most seismically active area, with an average of over 60 earthquakes a century (Richter 4).

2·2 The Caledonian Canal

The Great Glen fault is what made the Caledonian Canal possible. Only 22 miles of this historic waterway are man-made; the other 38 rely on the natural waterways of Lochs Lochy, Oich and Ness. The Great Glen Way clings closely to the canal route all the way from Corpach to Fort Augustus, but does not rejoin it until the final approach to Inverness.

The canal was first proposed in 1773, and was designed by two engineers, William Jessop and Thomas Telford, beginning in 1803. Jessop took on Telford, the son of a Dumfries-shire shepherd, as his assistant and although they worked on it jointly, Telford seems to be given most of the credit.

It was an ambitious venture, demanding the moving of huge amounts of material and creating work for up to 1200 labourers. Telford and Jessop had proposed a canal depth of 20 feet, but dredging problems restricted it to about 14 feet. It took 19 years to complete, and cost £912,000 - a huge sum of money at the time. There were great celebrations when it finally opened in 1822.

The canal was built mainly to create jobs and boost trade, but commercial use was never great, partly because of its limited depth. It was a lifeline for lochside communities in an era when roads were poor or absent. Later, it provided a safe passage, avoiding the Pentland Firth, for thousands of naval vessels during the first world war. Otherwise leisure craft became its main users. It was paid for entirely by public money, and remains the earliest example of nationalised transport in Britain.

The maximum size of ships that can navigate the canal is 35 foot beam by 150 foot long by 13.5 foot draught (or 160 foot long by 9 foot draught), and the speed limit is six miles per hour (10 kph). For contact details of boat charters, operating hours and regulations, see page 62.

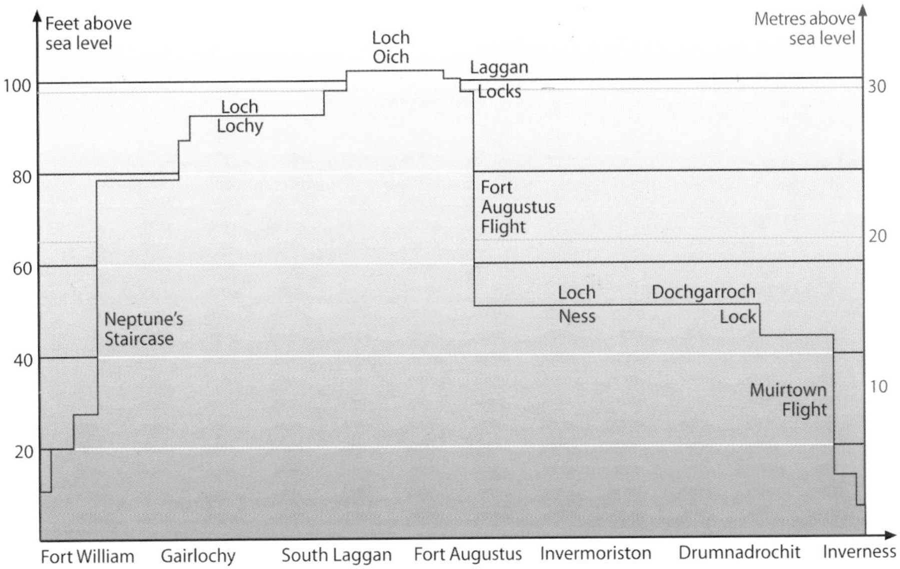

Its highest point is Loch Oich, at 106 feet (32 m) above sea level. Water drains from its southern end towards the Atlantic, and leaves its northern end towards the North Sea. Differences in level between the lochs are handled by 29 locks, each of which raises or lowers the level by up to eight feet. Watching the boats being worked through the locks adds interest to towpath walking.

Notice as you walk the Way that the lock gates open in the opposite direction after the watershed. Lock gates are always angled so that the pressure of water at the higher level holds them closed. This is obvious in the photographs of Muirtown Locks (page 21), and in Neptune's Staircase, a flight of locks which lifts boats by 64 feet (page 41).

Capstans were worked by leverage

Originally locks were worked by muscle power and leverage. The lock-keeper slotted a long wooden pole into each of the outward-facing sockets and rotated the capstan to open or close a lock gate. The poles were sometimes stored on top of the capstan in a tall pyramid supported by further sockets set into the top.

Cruiser heading through Kytra Lock

Although by 1968 all the locks had been mechanised, many of the capstans are still in place on the towpath. There is a good example, complete with poles, in the Canal Visitor Centre in Fort Augustus (page 47).

The canal has many other interesting features, including ten swing bridges and various weirs, aqueducts and tunnels. There are the distinctive pepper-pot lighthouses and beacons at Corpach, Gairlochy, Fort Augustus, Loch Dochfour (Bona) and at Clachnaharry, the sea lock at Inverness. Originally they were occupied and worked by lighthouse-keepers, but later all were automated.

Lock gates opening at Fort Augustus

Walking to the sea locks

Corpach sea lock with lighthouse

To see the Canal 'end-to-end', it's worth extending your walk to visit both sea locks. To reach Corpach lighthouse near Fort William is only a short diversion from the Way: see page 41.

At the Inverness end, you have to make more of an effort although you might halve the distance with a lift or a taxi to Muirtown Bridge. To walk there from Inverness Castle is about a mile by the simplest route (not the best, but easy to describe). Cross the River Ness just north of the castle, then turn third right up Kenneth Street which becomes Telford Street. This meets the canal at Muirtown Bridge, with locks to your left and a large boat basin to your right.

Muirtown Basin was large enough to serve as a second harbour to Inverness, but as ships became too big its use declined. There is a wall plaque that celebrates Telford's achievement with a poem by the then Poet Laureate, Robert Southey. The Muirtown workshops still serve the entire canal.

It's well worth walking a further mile along the towpath (along either side of Muirtown Basin) to reach Clachnaharry sea lock, built out into the Beauly Firth because of shallow water near the shore. Cross the railway line (with care: it's unsupervised) and walk all the way to the small beacon. There are great views of the Firth (keep an eye out for dolphins), Ben Wyvis to the north-west and the possible spectacle of boats arriving and leaving.

Cross the canal by a lock gate to return to Muirtown Bridge along the opposite side of the basin. If you have time in hand, you could add a 1-mile round trip north-east to the pier at South Kessock where a ferry used to ply until 1982.

Muirtown locks

2·3 Historical background

Hill forts of the Great Glen

Some ten hill-top forts testify to the Great Glen's strategic importance since the Iron Age. They may also have been used as a line-of-sight signalling system using beacons. The most accessible to Great Glen walkers are Torr Dhuin (from Fort Augustus) and Craig Phadrig (from Inverness). Dun Deardail is a small diversion off the West Highland Way to the south of Fort William, not to be confused with Dun Dearduil at Farigaig, near Foyers on the south shore of Loch Ness. The forts are worth visiting for the glorious views from their hill-top sites. Nearly all are owned by the Forestry Commission: for more information, visit the FC website or that of RCAHM: see pages 61 and 62.

Some of these forts are called vitrified (glassy) because of the shiny appearance of their stones after intense fires had partly melted them. Mystery surrounds the cause of these fires, whether deliberate or accidental, but they must have burned for long periods at extremely high temperatures.

Torr Dhuin stands above Kytra Lock, and you can reach it by a Forestry Commission waymarked trail in under an hour from its car park at Ardachy which is, however, some 4 km from Fort Augustus. The walk gives excellent views over Kytra Lock and towards the Corrieyairack Pass, but the fort itself is overgrown and you need a bit of imagination and background knowledge to make sense of what you see at ground level.

A walk to Craig Phadrig

For a clearer view of a hill fort itself, we recomment Craig Phadrig, a large oval structure sitting atop a splendid wooded crag at the western edge of Inverness. You could walk to it in about 40 minutes from Muirtown Bridge (see page 21). Alternatively, the no 14 bus (to Craig Dunain) goes from Church Street in the city centre to the foot of Leachkin Brae (pronounced *larkin bray*). From the car park, allow 45 minutes to an hour to enjoy the fort.

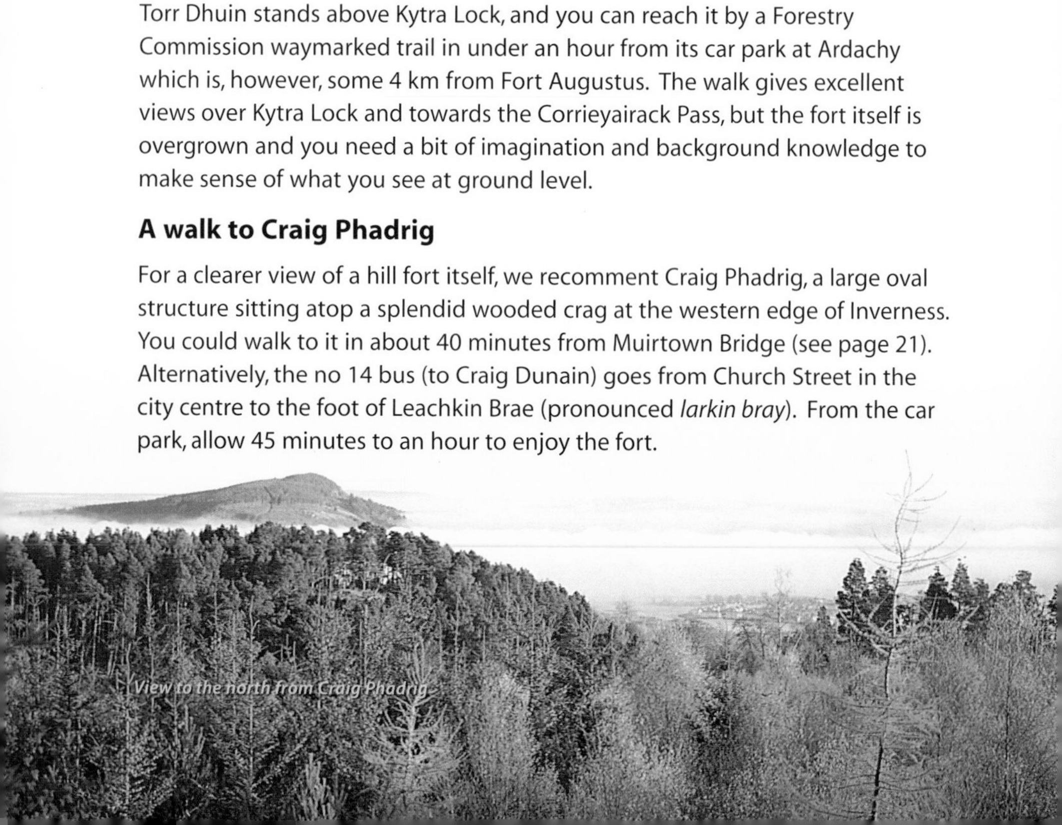

View to the north from Craig Phadrig

On foot from Muirtown Bridge, continue north-east to the junction and turn left along King Brude Road (which becomes General Booth Road). Take the third turning right (Leachkin Road) and go straight over the small roundabout. Turn second right up Leachkin Brae – a dead-end signposted for Upper Leachkin.

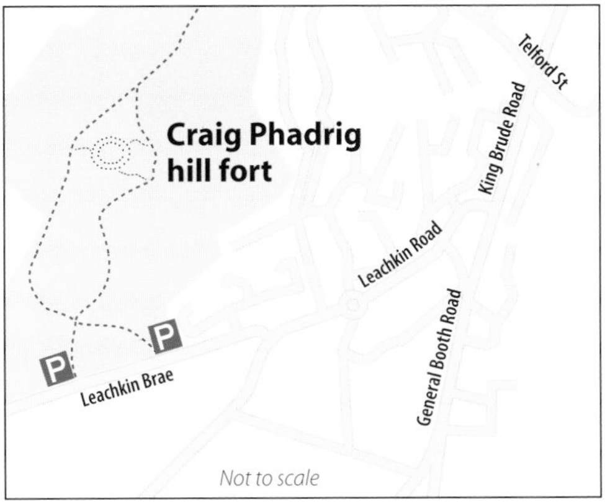

There are two car parks on the right of Leachkin Brae. From either, walk straight through the access gate at the back and follow the yellow marker posts. The paths join and then lead into the yellow waymarked route that encircles the fort. From several points on this you can climb through the woods to the hill-top (at about 575 ft/175 m). The Forestry Commission plans changes to both car parks and paths during 2006, so watch out for local signage and refer to the map above.

In 2005 there were only a couple of gaps in the trees, with tantalising glimpses of wonderful views to the south-west and east. The upgrade will probably include felling some non-native trees, extending these views. The photograph on page 22 shows the view to the north, taken in 1990.

The fort is overgrown with grass and scrub, but you can clearly see the two concentric oval ramparts, made of stones that once were interlaced with timber and vitrified (glassy) in places. Although the ramparts are now heavily grassed, stones still protrude in places and there's a vitrified section of inner rampart near a pine tree at its northern end. Originally the walls would have been massive – at least 26 feet high and 21 feet thick (8 m high by 6 m thick).

Radioactive carbon dating suggests that it was constructed around 350 BC. Although damaged by fire repeatedly, the site was occupied from time to time for many centuries and became a capital of the Pictish kings.

At the time of St Columba's missionary visit in 580 AD, the pagan King Brude refused him entry. According to legend, the gates mysteriously fell open when Columba knocked, and King Brude and his people were so impressed that they converted to Christianity. This hill was the origin of the city of Inverness.

The Jacobite risings and military roads

In 1688, James VII of Scotland (who was also James II of England) was deposed by popular demand, partly because he was thought to be promoting the Catholic Church. Parliament chose instead his daughter Mary, also of the house of Stewart, who had married the Dutch Protestant William of Orange.

After William and Mary came to the British throne (1688-9), those who supported the other Stewart line of James VII and his son James (the 'Old Pretender') became known as Jacobites: Jacobus is Latin for James. Queen Mary showed little interest in Scotland and her Dutch husband, William of Orange, was resented as a foreigner. The unpopularity of the 1707 Act of Union, together with the sense of distance from decisions made in London, gave the Jacobite cause a nationalist flavour.

During 1689-1745, contact was kept up between Scotland and the Jacobite court, first in France then Italy. The two famous Jacobite risings took place in 1715 and 1745. The 'Fifteen' focused on the Old Pretender, and the 'Forty-five' on his son, Charles Edward Stewart, also known as 'Bonnie Prince Charlie' or the 'Young Pretender'.

In 1746, the Battle of Culloden (see page 59) marked the final defeat of the Jacobites. Against advice, Bonnie Prince Charlie insisted on pitched battle on an open site unsuited to his highlanders' tactics. His army was hungry, sleepless and heavily outnumbered, and government troops led by 'Butcher' Cumberland routed them in under an hour. About 2000 Jacobites were killed in this battle, the last fought on British soil.

However, 'Bonnie Prince Charlie' remained in Scotland for another five months, living in hiding, being pursued all over the highlands and islands by the military. Famous among those who protected and helped him at this time is Flora Macdonald, whose statue stands outside Inverness Castle.

In the aftermath of Culloden, the government began a building programme to make troop movement around the Highlands easier. Barracks were built at Fort William, Fort Augustus and Fort George. A system of military roads and bridges were constructed, many of them still used by hikers today. The leading figure was General George Wade (1673-1748), an Irishman who served as Commander-in-Chief of the army in North Britain (Scotland) from 1724-40.

During that period, he built 240 miles of military roads, including the ones along the southern banks of Lochs Oich and Ness (1725-6) and the Corrieyairack Road. This stretches from Fort Augustus to Laggan and was built in 1731 by 500 soldiers. For over a century it was the highest maintained public road in Britain, rising to 2500 feet (770 m). Follow the directions on page 30 to walk to it from Fort Augustus. Wade also helped to plan the barracks at Fort Augustus.

Many of the works credited to Wade were actually built by William Caulfeild, who had been his deputy and was in charge from 1740-67. Wade and Caulfeild built roads to a standard width of six feet, with drainage ditches on either side. Wade's work is referred to as 'crushing rebellious Scots' in one (seldom sung) verse of Britain's national anthem.

The Corrieyairack Road from Meall a' Cholumain

2·4 Hill and mountain side-trips

This section explains the 'Munro terminology' for Scottish mountains, then recommends four hill climbs that you may want to include in your plans, weather permitting. The first two are from Fort William, followed by one each from Fort Augustus and Grotaig.

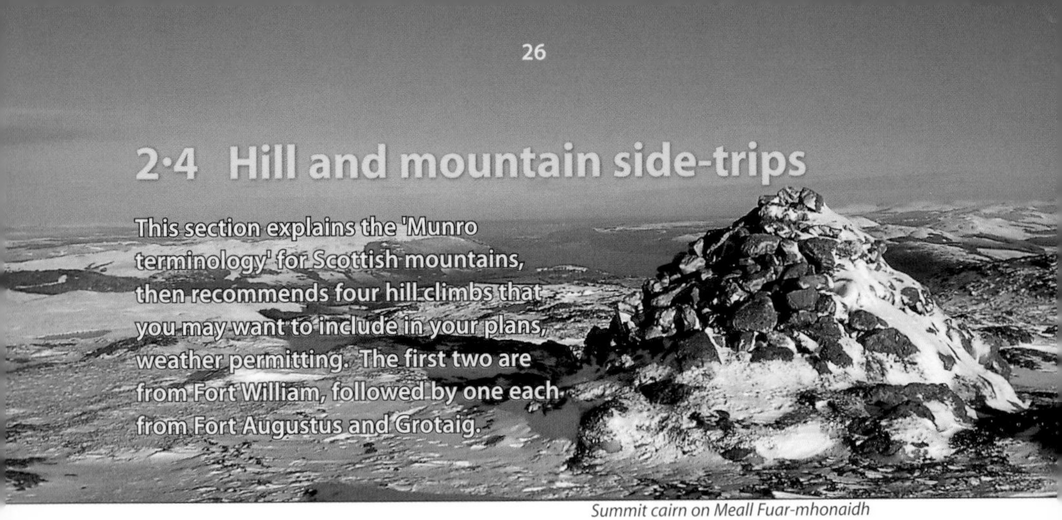

Summit cairn on Meall Fuar-mhonaidh

Munros, Corbetts and Grahams

A Munro is a Scottish mountain whose summit is over 3000 feet (914.4 m), provided its peak is separated from any neighbouring summits by a drop of at least 500 feet. Otherwise it is classified as a 'Top'.

Hugh Munro (1856-1919) was a London-born doctor who spent many years walking in the Scottish mountains. He was founder member of the Scottish Mountaineering Club (1889) and served as its President (1894-7). In Victorian times, many people believed that there were only about 30 peaks over 3000 feet, but Munro was convinced there were many more. His published table of 1891 listed 238 such peaks and 538 Tops. He was still working on a revised table when he died.

Although he did not climb all the mountains that he listed, Munro's work ignited a lively debate and launched what has now become the popular sport of 'Munro-bagging'. The first Munroist was the Reverend A E Robertson, who completed his final Munro (as then listed) in Glen Coe in 1901.

There has been debate about the total, and the exact distinction between a Munro and a Top, ever since. The generally accepted figure nowadays is 284 Munros and 511 Tops, the revised numbers reflecting more accurate survey methods (SMC 1997).

Some determined climbers ascend all the Munros in a single expedition lasting several months, whereas others spread the challenge over a lifetime. Charlie Campbell, a Glasgow postman, set a most impressive record of 48½ days in July 2000. At least 100 people become Munroists every year, and about 3400 had registered completion with the SMC by 2005. Since many more do not register, the true number will be much greater.

A Corbett is smaller: over 2500 feet (762 m) and with a drop of at least 500 feet all round. A Graham is smaller again, and, somewhat bizarrely, is defined metrically as over 610 m (2001 feet) and with a drop of at least 150 m (492 feet) all round.

Many fine mountains stand close to the Great Glen. There are two Munros above Loch Lochy: Sron a' Choire Ghairbh (935 m) and Meall na Teanga (917 m). A keen Munroist could take a day out from, say, Laggan Youth Hostel to bag either or both or these: see page 44 for brief notes. Here we focus on a few hills and mountaints that are feasible in the context of walking the Way.

Ben Nevis (1344 m) is the highest peak in Britain, and thus irresistible to many who stay in Fort William. Be clear, however, that this is a mountain climb, not a hill walk, and it needs an extra day as well as luck with the weather. In case you lack either of these, we also include Cow Hill (287 m), not only because it's much smaller but also because in dubious weather it will show you why the summit of Ben Nevis can be a dangerous place.

Our next suggestion is Meall a' Cholumain, a small hill above Fort Augustus, your half-way point and a fine place to take time out. Although at 315 m it's barely half the height of a Graham, it offers a splendid view in return for very modest effort, with historical interest en route.

On day four you could climb Meall Fuar-mhonaidh (699 m) a Graham that on a clear day gives sensational views from the Atlantic to the North Sea. The Way passes through Grotaig (page 52), which lacks only 420 m of altitude to its summit. The downside is that you are already committed to walking 14 miles (22 km) from Invermoriston to Drumnadrochit, and if you are carrying a heavy pack, this side-trip would make it a long, strenuous day. Read the description on page 31, and be prepared to turn back if conditions are poor.

Mountain Code

To report an accident in the Great Glen, telephone 01463 715555 (or 999).

Before you go

Learn to use a compass and map.

Know the weather signs and local forecast.

Plan within your abilities.

Know simple first aid and the symptoms of exposure.

Know the mountain distress signals.

When you go

Never go alone.

Leave a note of your route, and report on your return.

Take windproofs, waterproofs and survival bag.

Take suitable map and compass, torch and food.

Wear suitable boots.

Keep alert all day.

In winter

(November to March)

Each person needs an ice-axe and crampons, and to know how to use them.

Learn to recognise dangerous snow slopes.

Group members may need protection, such as climbing rope and technical gear.

Cow Hill (942 ft/287 m)

time **from 1½ to 3 hours, depending on start point (Lundavra Road or town centre), and whether you extend the walk to return via Glen Nevis**
terrain **good surface throughout**

Walk south-west from the town centre alongside the A82 and bear left up Lundavra Road at the roundabout. Follow it uphill until the road ends at a cattle grid. Immediately turn left through a gate up the signposted track. The path is tree-lined at first but soon emerges onto open hillside, climbing moderately through moorland.

Shortly after you start seeing views of the brooding massif of Ben Nevis, you reach a path junction marked with stone signs (25 minutes from the cattle grid). Turn left for Cow Hill. After a further 25 minutes you reach the hilltop mast, crossing a slight dip in the path before the final climb. The views over Fort William and Loch Linnhe are spectacular, with the start of the Caledonian Canal at Corpach to the north and River Lochy further to your right.

Return to the path junction and either retrace your steps to Lundavra Road or continue along the Peat Track (signposted for Glen Nevis) down through pine plantation to join the West Highland Way (within 1 km of the marked junction). This soon meets the Glen Nevis road, where you turn left for Fort William.

Ben Nevis (4406 ft/1344m)

time **5 to 7½ hours depending on your fitness**
terrain **well surfaced pony track**

Before committing yourself to 'The Ben', review your fitness, experience and the weather forecast. If in doubt, we suggest Cow Hill might be a better choice. However, in good conditions, any fit walker can manage the long, strenuous slog up the pony track. Be aware of the dangers posed by poor visibility on the summit plateau (see panel) and be prepared to turn back if need be.

Take extra warm clothing and food in addition to your standard walking gear and waterproofs. There are on average 261 gales per annum, with more than 157 inches of precipitation on the summit and yes, it can snow even in summer. Take a compass and large-scale map (Harvey's 1:25,000 is ideal) and if you don't know how to use them, go with somebody who does. Request the free MCofS leaflet *Navigation on Ben Nevis*: see page 61 for a website source.

The zig-zag pony track was built to service the observatory that worked on the summit from 1883-1904. Please stick closely to its line: taking short-cuts leads to erosion and can disturb ground-nesting birds.

Start from Achintee Farm, 2 km south-east of Fort William. Alternatively, follow the West Highland Way to the Glen Nevis Visitor Centre and cross River Nevis by footbridge. The track steadily climbs the lower shoulder of Meall an t-Suidhe (711 m) for about a mile before the track from Glen Nevis youth hostel joins it from the right. From here on, the gradient increases as it curves anticlockwise around the shoulder and approaches Lochan Meall an t-Suidhe at the col.

Turn sharply south at the track junction and cross the Red Burn in a deep gully: at 675 m you have reached the half-way point, a good place to review progress and conditions. If all is well, continue up the long series of steep zig-zags to gain the lunar landscape of the summit plateau.

Sadly, people still die on the Ben, caught by worsening weather and confusion on the summit cliffs. If you have any doubts by the halfway point (Red Burn Ford), turn back. In bad weather, the only safe escape route is to walk from the trig pillar 150 metres along a grid bearing of 231°, then follow 282° to clear the plateau. Unless you are competent with a compass, and can correct magnetic bearings, don't risk it.

Cliffs on the Ben's summit drop 2000 feet

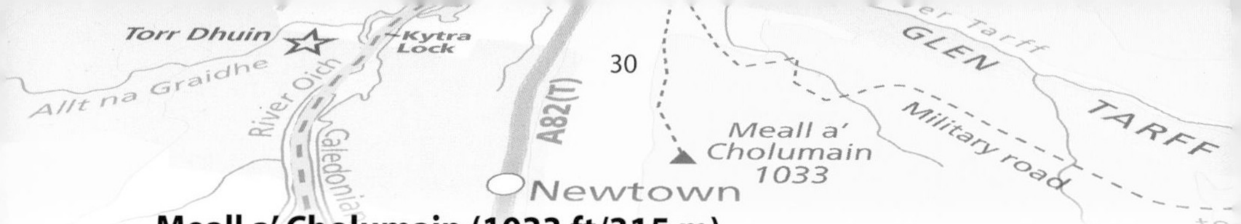

Meall a' Cholumain (1033 ft/315 m)

time **2½-3 hours from the village centre or 1½-2 hours from the minor road**
terrain **sound surface (4x4 road) except for summit area (boggy)**

From Fort Augustus, walk south-west alongside the A82 main road and at the caravan park cross the road to follow the sign 'Footpath to burial ground'.

Turn left up a bumpy, grassy road and enter Kilchumein cemetery through the gate. It has several graves with literary connections, and many of soldiers wounded and gassed in the First World War. Cross the cemetery diagonally to the far corner wall and climb over using the protruding stone steps.

Follow the path for 300 m until it reaches a minor public road where you turn right. Walk along the road for 700 m, almost returning to the A82, but turn left at a gate to follow the Corrieyairack Road. (A lift to this point from Fort Augustus would save about 3 km, but there is nowhere to park a car.)

Pass through the gate with its sign warning against damage to General Wade's Road, a scheduled ancient monument: see page 25 for background. It is narrow and boulder-strewn at first, but after the entrance to Culachy Farm it becomes broader and is used by farm vehicles. The obstacles in the first section are to prevent people from driving their 4x4 vehicles all the way through from Laggan.

Follow the military road uphill for about 20 minutes, then go through a gate in a deer fence and, soon after, pass under power lines. About 250 m beyond the power lines the path divides. The military road bears left, snaking uphill towards the pass. Bear right towards the hill-top mast that marks your destination.

The track becomes steeper after you pass the ruined croft at Knollbuck, but the surface remains good, and it's still used by maintenance vehicles. The mast stands on a flat, featureless hilltop with a good view to the right over Fort Augustus and up Loch Ness, with Meall Fuar-mhonaidh dominating the skyline.

Be sure to continue south-west for 5 minutes across the peat and heather (which may be boggy underfoot) for an even better view. Below and to your left lies the charming Loch Oich, beyond it the broader expanse of Loch Lochy with Loch Linnhe in the distance and dramatic peaks to the north: see page 47.

Retrace your steps to the minor road and return to Fort Augustus either by retracing your steps or, if you have a map, continue along the minor road until you cross River Tarff and bear left, then right, to return via the B862.

Meall Fuar-mhonaidh (2293 feet/699 m)

time **about 3½ hours round trip**

terrain **well-defined path but boggy, sometimes very boggy, especially during or after heavy rain**

The Way climbs to Grotaig car park on a track which meets a minor road along which the Way continues to the right. To climb the mountain, turn left briefly to a track on the right signposted 'Hill Walk' and go through the gate. The path runs between Grotaig Burn and a fence, through mixed woodland rich in bird life. The going can be boggy in places, but some sections have been improved by boardwalk. After several stiles you reach one marked with a notice warning about conditions on the 'mountain path'.

An abrupt change of vegetation confirms that the climb begins in earnest, as you emerge onto open hillside covered in bell and ling heather. At first it ascends gently, then swings north to climb more steeply. You reach a tall stile over a deer fence, with a warning notice about stalking (August to February).

Ascend through increasingly exposed moorland, across peat bog and some rocky ground, the gradient varying from gentle to fairly steep. You walk along a low, rounded ridge, with great views over Loch Ness to your left and the hills and moorland to your right. The path is always well-defined, albeit sometimes braided where walkers have taken different routes to avoid the boggiest bits.

The final half-hour's climb is heralded by a dip in the path, with some very boggy bits. The first cairn you reach is a false summit: just beyond it there's a wonderful view to the south-west over Lochs Lochy and Oich. Continue west for a further 10 minutes to reach the true summit cairn, the highest of four in the summit plateau: see the photograph on page 26.

On a clear day, you can see all the way from Loch Linnhe beyond Fort William to the Moray Firth beyond Inverness. There's a strong sense of how the Great Glen cuts a swathe through the Highlands, from the Atlantic Ocean to the North Sea. Retrace your steps to Grotaig.

2·5 Habitats and wildlife

Salmon leaping upstream

The Great Glen Way runs through three main types of habitat, described below:

- water-side
- woodland
- heath and moorland.

If you are really keen to spot wildlife, carry binoculars and walk alone, or seek fellow-walkers who share your interest and are willing to keep quiet when it matters. Try to set off soon after sunrise, or go for a stroll in the evening. Animals are much more active at these times than in the middle of the day. Since this applies to midges too, protect your skin thoroughly, especially from May to September and in still weather.

Water-side

Much of the Way lies near water, along man-made canal and the rivers and lochs. Look out for insects, birds and perhaps some small mammals.

Near Corpach, look for oystercatchers in the fields. Their strong orange bills are good at cracking open cockles and mussels, and they are easy to spot. When in flight, their wings show an obvious white-on-black M-shape, and their piercing cries are unmistakeable.

Oystercatcher

You are likely to see Britain's most widespread bird of prey, the kestrel. It feeds on small mammals, mainly field voles and mice: its excellent eyesight lets it detect their tiny movements in the grass, and it hunts in a fast dive with half-closed wings. Recognise it by its ability to hover and its pointed chestnut-coloured wings.

Because the Great Glen is open to the sea at both ends, some sea birds use it as a corridor. You may see wandering seabirds such as kittiwakes, guillemots, fulmars and shearwaters in the heart of the glen. Look for cormorants hanging out their wings to dry, especially at Invermoriston pier. For wildlife in Loch Ness, see page 15; keep a look-out for anything unexpected on or in the water.

Look out for grey heron hunting for fish and frogs: sometimes they stand tall and motionless in the shallows, at other times they stalk their prey. In flight, they trail their legs and their huge grey wings beat very slowly.

If you are very lucky, you might see the magnificent osprey diving talons first to carry off a fish. Rescued from extinction in Britain, the osprey population has slowly grown in the highlands since the first pair returned to Loch Garten in 1955. They are visitors, over-wintering in West Africa and returning each spring, often to the same nesting site. Ospreys have established several new nest sites in the Great Glen over the last ten years.

Osprey lifting its prey out of the loch torpedo-style

Pine martens depend on woodland habitats

Woodland

The Great Glen is richly wooded, with a mixture of native species (broad-leaved and pine) and productive conifers. These woodlands also provide food, nesting sites and shelter for wildlife.

In prehistoric times, Scotland was covered by natural mixed woodlands known as the ancient Caledonian forest. On the lower and south-facing slopes, birch, oak, ash, cherry, hazel and rowan flourished. Birch were also successful on the higher ground, along with Scots pine, juniper and other hardy species. In the wetter areas, willow and alder predominated.

Over the last 4000-5000 years, humans cleared this forest to make way for crops, animal grazing or the planting of other tree species. However, remnants of the Caledonian forest survive and you still see ancient oakwoods, for example on the slopes of Loch Ness. Native pinewoods support many rare birds, including crested tit, Scottish crossbill and siskin (see page 35).

The pine marten became almost extinct in Britain and is therefore protected. Its rapid population rise in the Great Glen reflects the increase in woodland. It is the only predator agile enough to catch red squirrels.

Crested tit perching on Scots pine

Look for wood ants and their huge nests in the forest above Loch Ness near Grotaig. Tread carefully and please do not disturb them, as they occupy a niche in the food chain.

The productive forests in the Great Glen are dominated by non-native species, eg Douglas fir, Norway spruce, lodgepole pine and larch (European, Japanese and hybrid). These woods are an important habitat: big birds such as osprey, buzzard and goshawk need big trees in which to nest.

The siskin flourishes in pinewoods

The Forestry Commission (FC) owns most of the forests that you walk through, and enlightened planting policies have made for more diversity, not only in species, but also in the age structure of the tree population, with clear felling sometimes avoided, and two trees planted for every one felled. There is a target of 20% open space in newly planted areas. These policies are aimed at supporting all the wildlife niches in a sustainable way.

The FC also takes an active role in conservation. Scotland has 75% of the British red squirrel population, but on the south side of Loch Ness squirrels were being run over when crossing the road. The FC solution was to suspend bridges of thick rope 16 feet high above the roads, and grateful squirrels now use these rope bridges.

Red squirrel on rope bridge

Sika deer browse on Norway spruce

Three kinds of deer live in woodland, of which only red and roe deer are native. Sika deer were introduced into deer parks from Japan as recently as 1870; some escaped and bred successfully in the highlands, despite the harsh climate. They are difficult to spot because they stand motionless when frightened and prefer dense woodland. During the rut, sika stags make an eerie whistling noise.

Heath and moorland

Examples of Scots pine are found in this peaty moorland. After the Ice Age, 8 to 10 thousand years ago, Scots pine re-colonised the Great Glen; it is the only pine tree native to Britain. Isolated trees are useful perches for birds of prey.

Look up and you may see kestrel, buzzard or merlin. Birds of prey such as owls depend on small mammals for their diet. The field vole lives on grass, plants and fruit, and eight different birds prey on it. As much as 90% of the barn owl's diet consists of field voles.

Buzzards are much larger than owls, and are also known as 'the tourist's eagle', because visitors so often mistake them for eagle. The golden eagle's wing-span is over six feet, double the buzzard's, and it is confined to more remote areas: consider yourself very lucky if you see one.

Mature Scots pine has a distinctive shape

Skylarks have suffered badly on farmland elsewhere, but they flourish in the Great Glen. If you hear a call like the whistle of a boiling kettle, look for curlew, which has a long curved bill.

On higher ground, watch and listen for grouse (red and black). You might see ptarmigan, a mountain grouse whose body feathers turn white in winter.

If you see pathways of nibbled heather and blaeberry, look for mountain hare, which also turns white in winter. Even in their brown coats, the mountain hare looks different from its brown cousin: its ears are much shorter and its tail lacks the black tip.

Hare predators include the fox and golden eagle. (There are very few rabbits in the Great Glen.) A healthy population of mountain hare may help eagles to sustain two chicks per year. Via the mountain hare, the heather thus supports the golden eagle that soars above it.

Mountain hare

Owls prey on voles and mice

3·1 The starting-point: Fort William

The town's original fort, a crude structure, was built in 1654-5 by General Monk. It was replaced by a stone garrison for 100 soldiers built in 1690 by General Mackay, who named it after William III (William of Orange). Ever since, the settlement, formerly called Inverlochy, has been known as Fort William.

Although the fort withstood many conflicts, it later fell into disuse. In 1889 the land was bought by the West Highland Railway Company, which built its railway over part of the fort. The little that has survived is at the starting-point of the Way, with the stone marker standing amid its ruins: see photograph on page 4.

Fort William is a major centre for tourism in the west Highlands, and a popular base for hikers and climbers. It is dominated by Britain's highest mountain, Ben Nevis: see page 28. Glen Nevis offers superb hiking, with its waterfalls, a precarious three-string bridge and a wealth of wild flowers and birds. The Visitor Centre is open daily from Easter to late October (tel 01397 705 922).

The West Highland Museum has information about the town and its fortifications. It's open year-round Monday to Saturday, also on Sunday afternoons in July/August (tel 01397 702 169), and the Tourist Information Centre is nearby. There's also a good range of outdoor equipment shops.

There is an interesting boat trip to Seal Island, with daily sailings April-October from the Town Pier: tel 01397 703 919. Try to go at low tide, when more seals will be basking. Two miles north-east of the town on the A82, the Ben Nevis distillery has a visitor centre, offers tours and tastings, and is open Monday to Saturday, Easter to October (tel 01397 700 200).

Ben Nevis dominates Fort William

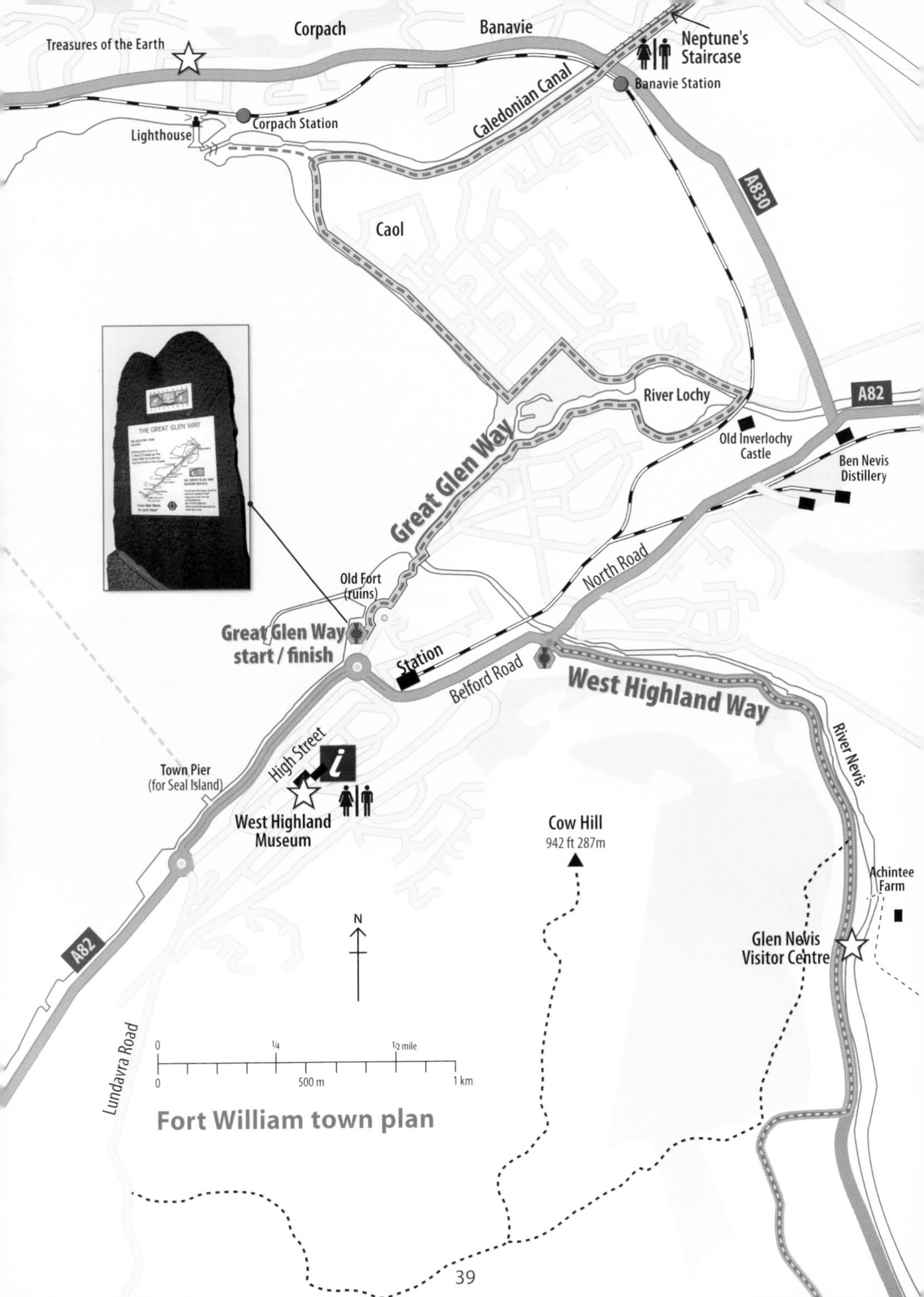
Corpach
Banavie
Treasures of the Earth
Neptune's Staircase
Banavie Station
Caledonian Canal
Corpach Station
Lighthouse
A830
Caol
THE GREAT GLEN WAY
River Lochy
A82
Old Inverlochy Castle
Ben Nevis Distillery
Great Glen Way
North Road
Old Fort (ruins)
Great Glen Way start / finish
Station
Belford Road
West Highland Way
High Street
i
River Nevis
Town Pier (for Seal Island)
West Highland Museum
Cow Hill
942 ft 287m
Achintee Farm
N
Glen Nevis Visitor Centre
A82
Lundavra Road
0
1/4
1/2 mile
0
500 m
1 km
Fort William town plan

3·2 Fort William to Gairlochy

Map	**panel 1 (outside back cover)**
Distance	**10 miles (16 km)**
Terrain	**pavement at first, then riverside path, more pavement, with the remainder being canal towpath**
Grade	**very easy**
Food and drink	**Fort William, Caol, Banavie**
Side-trips	**Old Inverlochy Castle, Corpach sea lock**
Summary	**easy walking, enlivened by many interesting canal features including Neptune's Staircase, and views of Ben Nevis**

Across Corpach sea lock to Ben Nevis

Old Inverlochy Castle *is one of Scotland's earliest stone castles, built by Sir John Comyn, Black Lord of Badenoch. The site had been fortified since AD 273. The castle was built in 1260 as a square with 9-foot thick walls and a round tower at each corner. Open daily year-round.*

Old Inverlochy Castle

If arriving by train, follow waymarkers from the station diagonally across the supermarket car park and over the main road. Divert briefly left to the stone marker that defines the Way's terminus. Just before you cross the River Lochy, visit Old Inverlochy Castle, where an information board tells you about its history and famous battles.

Neptune's Staircase, a flight of eight locks

After the castle, walk along the pavement through Caol to reach the Caledonian Canal. Before turning right to follow the Way, divert left for 300 yards to Corpach sea lock, with its lock-keepers' cottages and pepper-pot lighthouse: see the red line on the town plan (page 39).

Return to the towpath, skirting around Banavie (**ban**avee) Station and passing by Neptune's Staircase: see page 19. Follow the towpath all the way to Gairlochy, enjoying superb views across to the ski slopes of Aonach Mor.

The scenery becomes increasingly rural, with a fine variety of trees and splendid views of the mountains. After 4 miles (6.5 km) you reach the historic swing bridge of Moy, where each half has to be opened separately. Within a mile, you arrive at the small village of Gairlochy.

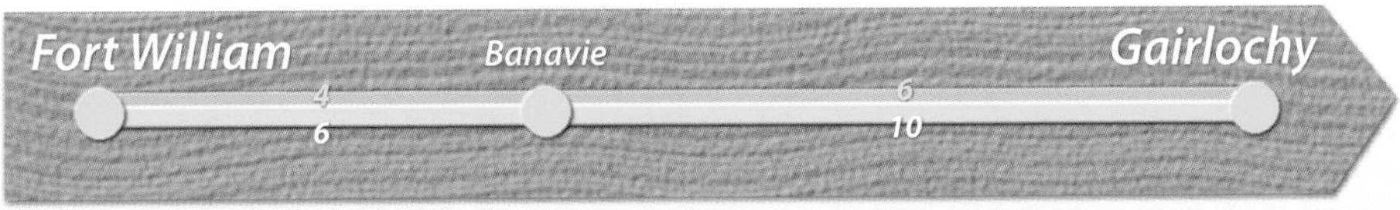

3·3 Gairlochy to South Laggan

Map	panels 1 and 2 (outside back cover)
Distance	13 miles (21 km)
Terrain	a mix of tarmac and forest paths and tracks, mostly shared with the Great Glen Cycle Route
Grade	mainly easy, with two short steep ascents
Food and drink	Great Glen Water Park (Loch Oich-side)
Side-trips	Clan Cameron Museum (Achnacarry), Cia-aig waterfall
Summary	fairly easy walking along the length of Loch Lochy, with splendid views

Looking towards Laggan Locks from above Kilfinnan

Clan Cameron Museum, Achnacarry

In this section, you walk through land owned by the Camerons of Lochiel. Two miles after Gairlochy, there is the option of a small diversion to their museum, which you can combine with visiting the Cia-aig (pronounced Kaig) waterfall to rejoin the Way at Clunes. Bonnie Prince Charlie hid in a cave here for two weeks after his flight from Culloden.

> ***The Clan Cameron Museum***
>
> *covers the history of the clan and its Jacobite links, and has also photographs and reminders from the commando training era. It is open afternoons daily from April to October, also late mornings in July/August (tel 01397 712 480). Continue past the museum and cross the white bridge to reach the tip of Loch Arkaig. Turn right along the B8005 and near the hump-backed bridge look for where the waters of the Cia-aig fall into the Witch's Cauldron. Return along the Dark Mile (Mile Dorcha) to Clunes.*

Achnacarry House has belonged to the Camerons since 1660, but was destroyed in 1746 to punish them for their role in the Jacobite rising. This was the last place where clan chiefs used the pit and gallows to punish cattle stealers. The House was damaged in the second world war but was rebuilt afterwards.

Allow an extra 2-3 hours for this option at a moderate pace. Spare a thought for the Commando recruits who in wartime, heavily laden, had to complete a five-mile round trip in under 50 minutes. From 1942-45, Achnacarry housed the British Commando Basic Training Centre, which put 25,000 recruits through extremely tough training. Some recruits died because of a realistic regime using live ammunition. The memorial near Spean Bridge honours their memory: see page 44.

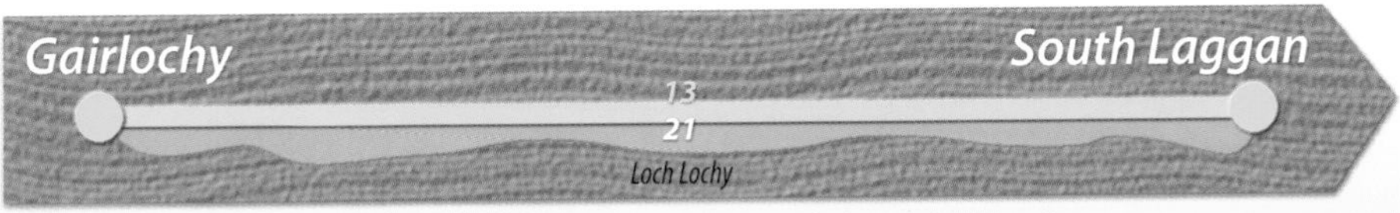

From Clunes all the way to Kilfinnan, you walk on forest tracks, punctuated by splendid views of Loch Lochy with mountains behind – including two Munros, see note below. The cemetery at Kilfinnan has a large mausoleum for the chiefs of Glengarry. Most of this section is shared with the Mountain Bike Route, so be aware of cycle traffic.

The last section from Kilfinnan to Laggan Locks is on a minor road. You are close to the site of the Battle of the Shirts in July 1544. This was a clan battle between the Frasers on one side and the ranks of Camerons, MacDonalds and MacDonnells on the other. It acquired its strange name from the unusually warm weather: so hot was the sunshine that the men removed their plaids and fought wearing only their undershirts.

Commando memorial, overlooking Spean Bridge

Laggan has a Youth Hostel but no refreshments. A mile further on, however, the Great Glen Water Park's coffee shop and restaurant is open daily year-round. It also provides accommodation (mainly by the week) and offers a wide range of water sports and other activities (telephone 01809 501 381).

Note on the two Munros above Loch Lochy

To climb Sron a' Choire Ghairbh (935 m) and Meall na Teanga (917 m) you'd need a full day to spare, suitable equipment and experience. Refer to the Mountain Code on page 27, carry a detailed map and compass and be prepared to turn back if conditions worsen.

You would start from the high track south-west half a mile short of Kilfinnan, where a sign points to 'Tomdoun (Cam Bhealach)'. After a couple of miles walking south-westerly, parallel to Loch Lochy, you strike west to the summit of the bhealach (pass), following the Allt Glas Dhoire upstream. From the pass, you can climb either Munro, but you would have to double-back to bag both. The classic approach (a through traverse of both peaks, starting from near Clunes and ending at Kilfinnan) needs support from a car driver.

3·4 South Laggan to Invermoriston

Map	**panels 2 and 3**
Distance	**18 miles (29 km)**
Terrain	**some tarmac, railway track-bed, old military road, then canal towpath to Fort Augustus; afterwards forest track almost to Invermoriston (beware bicycles)**
Grade	**easy to Fort Augustus; noticeable gradients thereafter**
Food and drink	**Laggan Swing Bridge (shop), Great Glen Water Park, Fort Augustus, Invermoriston**
Side-trips	**Fort Augustus (various, see page 47)**
Summary	**scenic sections along Loch Oich-side and past Kytra Lock, with mixed woodland and lovely views; break this section overnight in Fort Augustus if possible**

From South Laggan to Aberchalder, you walk along the canalside through the tall trees of Laggan avenue and near a small stone church, both established by Thomas Telford.

At Laggan swing bridge, you have the option of a diversion to visit the macabre Well of the Seven Heads or to buy supplies at the shop. Otherwise, carry on past the Great Glen Water Park and into the Leiterfearn nature reserve and enjoy the wonderful ash, birch, elm and hazel woodland, with primrose and dog violets beneath.

At the start of the forest you may notice a wall, a relic of old Invergarry station, a stop on the ill-fated railway whose trackbed you now join. Trains used to run between Spean Bridge and Fort Augustus, but the line was abandoned in 1911, a casualty of rivalry and treachery between competing railway companies. Although briefly reprieved by popular demand, it finally closed in 1946.

River Oich at Fort Augustus

After a while, the trackbed gives way to General Wade's military road. Looking west across Loch Oich you may glimpse the ruins of Invergarry Castle, once the seat of the MacDonnells. Like many of the Great Glen clans, they supported the Jacobite cause. Bonnie Prince Charlie stayed there twice, and the castle was burned after Culloden.

At Aberchalder, notice the splendid old Bridge of Oich, designed by James Dredge in 1850. Its chains taper elegantly towards the middle, and the double-cantilever design means that each half is self-supporting. It carried cars until 1932.

The gentle descent from Aberchalder to Fort Augustus is perhaps the most secluded stretch of canal, through splendid mixed woodland and past delightful Kytra Lock. In places you walk along a narrow causeway, the canal to your right and the River Oich, more often heard than seen, to your left.

Before Kytra, the canal broadens into a narrow but natural loch. Look up to your left to see the Iron Age fort Torr Dhuin perched above: see page 22. Look right to locate the summit mast of Meall a' Cholumain, a rewarding walk described on page 30. The photographs on the title page and pp 47 and 25 were all taken from this climb.

Well of the Seven Heads

This 1812 monument is a reminder of a gruesome clan massacre in 1663. Following a dispute with the MacDonnells over succession, two Keppochs were killed, allegedly by accident. In retaliation, the Keppochs then killed seven MacDonnells, allegedly the murderers, in their own homes. Ian Lom MacDonald washed the severed heads in this well before taking them to Invergarry Castle to show them to his chieftain as proof.

Bridge of Oich

Fort Augustus

The locks, Fort Augustus

Originally known as Kilcumein, the village was renamed in 1729 by General Wade in honour of William Augustus, Duke of Cumberland. Midway between Fort William and Fort George, Fort Augustus was built in 1729 and became the hub of Wade's network of military roads.

The fort housed troops long after Culloden, but in 1867 it was sold to the Lovat family, descendants of an executed Jacobite. The 15th Lord Lovat gave it to Benedictine monks who adapted it for use first as a monastery, then as a school and from 1882 as an abbey. After the abbey closed in 1998 the monks moved to Pluscarden, and by 2005 it was being developed into a leisure complex with 91 luxury flats and 12 cottages.

Fort Augustus has many attractions, notably the sight of boats working through the flight of locks at its centre. Visit the Caledonian Canal Heritage Centre, on the north side of the canal (open April-October, admission free, tel 01320 366 493).

You can also cruise Loch Ness with sonar from here, from March to November; contact Cruise Loch Ness at 01320 366 221. The Forestry Commission has produced leaflets with forest walks, including one to Torr Dhuin: see page 22.

The view south-west from Meall a'Cholumain

The falls of Moriston

You leave Fort Augustus with a short, steep climb on a minor road that then levels out for a mile or so before it descends again almost to the A82. It then veers sharply away from it to climb through a forest of birch and pine, beside a stream and uphill to a forest track where it turns parallel to Loch Ness. There are good views back over the town with its locks and abbey.

Below you, unseen, is Loch Ness's only 'island' – actually a man-made crannog. Originally called Eilean Muireach, it was renamed Cherry Island by Oliver Cromwell, though its trees are tall pines. A crannog is an artificial Iron Age island made by piling up stones on the loch bed to make a foundation for a timber house, often on wooden stilts, so as to be secure from enemies. This one was identified only in 1908 when an intrepid Benedictine monk from Fort Augustus Abbey explored it, using diving gear borrowed from canal workers.

This section undulates through coniferous forest, with a wide variety of species and ages. From time to time you glimpse superb views across Loch Ness through the gaps in the forest.

Within a few miles, you glimpse the tiny village of Invermoriston below. Sadly for walkers' morale, the Way then heads up the Glen Moriston forest road, away from the village, before zigzagging down again.

The River Moriston tumbles down to Loch Ness through spectacular rocks near the splendid old bridge, which was designed by Thomas Telford. It was begun in 1805, one of a thousand built in the early 19th century. Its design was sound enough, but there were problems both with its construction and spiralling costs. The businessman who financed it was bankrupt before its completion in 1813. The bridge was restored many times, but after flood damage in 1951, it was replaced by the modern bridge (1954). This gives a good vantage point for admiring the older Telford design.

Glen Moriston timber has had economic value since the 13th century when ships were built from its oak and pine to go on the Crusades. Much later, trees were also floated downstream for use in constructing the Caledonian Canal. Hydro-electric power is produced by the Dundreggan dam and power station.

The old bridge at Invermoriston

3·5 Invermoriston to Drumnadrochit

Map	panels 3 and 4 (inside back cover)
Distance	14 miles (22 km)
Terrain	mainly forest tracks, a few miles along and beside a minor road, finally alongside the A82
Grade	mainly moderate with some steep sections
Food and drink	none between Invermoriston and Drumnadrochit
Side-trips	Urquhart Castle, Loch Ness Visitor Centres (two), Loch Ness cruises (various)
Summary	fine forest section above the loch-side, then plateau moorland and farmland with views over the Great Glen

South-west across Loch Ness to Meall Fuar-mhonaidh

Invermoriston to Drumnadrochit

Out of Invermoriston, the Way climbs high above Loch Ness, follows a short section of footpath, then generally rises to Grotaig. For much of this section you are on steeply undulating forest tracks, sometimes high above the loch, with splendid views, twice descending almost to the road. The forest has hidden interest, with trees surrounding a fine old packhorse bridge just downstream of where you cross the Allt Saigh.

There is a picnic table and car park at Grotaig. From here, keen hillwalkers may wish to climb Meall Fuar-mhonaidh: see page 31. Pronounced (roughly) **fur**vanie, its distinctive rounded summit is a landmark for miles around, from which on a clear day you can see the entire Great Glen from Ben Nevis to Inverness.

Follow the minor road for several miles across the plateau, using the roadside footpath where available. There are good views of Loch Ness to the south-west and Ben Wyvis to the north. John Cobb chose this stretch of the loch for his attempt on the water speed record in 1952. Far below you, beside the A82, there's a memorial to his death in the attempt.

Looking north across Loch Ness

You turn left off the road to descend to the River Coiltie, then walk down a gravel road. The Way meets the A82. Turn left across the river at Lewiston and (unless staying in Lewiston) follow the roadside path to reach Drumnadrochit.

The Way approaches Urquhart Bay Woods, a flat area of alder swamp around the estuaries of the Rivers Enrick and Coiltie – a Site of Special Scientific Interest. You can easily explore this on foot: at the crossroads near the Coiltie bridge, head east down the road to the Old Kilmore cemetery and climb steps over a wall beside its entrance. The track through the woods is waymarked. The last section, before it emerges at the shores of Loch Ness, is prone to flooding so waterproof footwear is advisable.

Drumnadrochit

Drumnadrochit is known locally as 'Drum'. Combined with neighbouring Lewiston, its population is about 1500. Although a smallish place, it hosts a number of visitor attractions and has a good network of local woodland paths, including Craigmonie Woods. Ask at the Tourist Information Centre for the leaflet *Paths around Dumnadrochit*, which also covers Urquhart Bay Woods.

Drum is famous as the capital of the monster industry. Its two Loch Ness visitor centres are strangely labelled 'official' and 'original'. Don't be put off by the floating Nessie model in the lochan outside the 'official' Loch Ness 2000 – it's well worth a visit for its open-ended approach to the evidence. You walk through six themed areas that present multimedia findings from the explorations. It attracts 200,000 visitors per annum and houses a field centre with educational and scientific goals. The project supports an informative website (page 62) and loch cruises, and the centre is open daily year-round (telephone 01456 450 573).

The 'original' Loch Ness Visitor Centre shows a film, has an exhibition and also offers loch cruises (open daily, telephone 01456 450 342). Also in the village centre is Castle Cruises (Art Gallery, March-December, telephone 01456 450 695).

Urquhart Castle

Urquhart Castle

Urquhart (pronounced **Urk**hurt) enjoys a majestic situation, commanding fine views along Loch Ness in both directions. It was built around 1250 on the site of an Iron Age fort, for Alan Durward, Lord of Urquhart and son-in-law of King Alexander II. The castle was taken from the English by William Wallace, but Edward I's soldiers recaptured it after a long siege in 1303.

The castle was seized in 1395 by Donald Macdonald, Lords of the Isles, and was besieged, raided and changed hands many times in the 14th to 16th centuries, notably in the Great Raid of 1545. It was disputed by the Jacobites in 1689, and partly blown up by government troops when they left in 1692. Sadly it was never repaired and much of its stone, timber and lead was plundered as building material.

Many of the present buildings are 17th century onward, although earlier parts also survive. The castle was used as a fortress and a residence for over 400 years. Its best-preserved part is the five-storey tower house built in the 16th century by Sir John Grant and known as the Grant Tower.

The castle suffers from its own popularity, drawing about 250,000 tourists per annum, mostly in the summer months. To enjoy it without the crowds, time your visit carefully, preferably for early morning on a weekday.

Urquhart Castle and Visitor Centre

The castle and its modern visitor centre are managed by Historic Scotland. The theatre shows a short video on its history, and there are also a shop, museum and café. Admission charge (£6 per adult in 2005) applies even to café. Open daily year-round (shorter hours in winter), telephone 01456 450 551.

3·6 Drumnadrochit to Inverness

Map	**panels 4 and 5 (inside back cover)**
Distance	**18 miles (29 km)**
Terrain	**mainly forest and moorland tracks, with several miles on a minor road and finally island and roadside paths**
Grade	**steep as far as Corryfoyness, then mainly moderate; then a significant descent to the outskirts of Inverness**
Food and drink	**none between Drumnadrochit and Inverness**
Summary	**the most challenging section of the Way, with some spectacular views, concluding at Inverness Castle**

River Ness

This is a long day, but very varied, with a mixture of farmland, exposed high moorland and woodland, finishing with the rural paths of Ness Islands leading to the grand setting of Inverness Castle.

You leave Drumnadrochit alongside the busy A82, but within two miles you start to climb away from it, opposite Temple Pier and up past Tychat. Look back for your last views over Urquhart Castle and the loch, perhaps glimpsing Meall Fuar-mhonaidh to the south-west. You climb through dense conifers to meet a wide forest road at Corryfoyness, a moorland farm.

The forest road climbs to the highest point so far (1250 feet/380 m), then descends slightly to meet another forest road near Achpopuli, where you turn right (north north-east). You are near Abriachan (ab**ree**achan), the tiny centre of Britain's largest community forest, and you pass its picnic area and car park with eco-toilet. In 1995 the Trust bought 403 acres of woodland from the Forestry Commission, and with strong local participation it manages the forest for wildlife and community benefit, creating marked trails, newsletters and a book.

You meet a minor road that leads past Loch Laide (pronounced **latch**ee), famous for its very pure water. Cross straight over it and continue for a mile beyond the road. Here the Way turns left along the minor road to Blackfold.

It's worth turning sharp right first, making a 500-yard diversion to see the Caiplich prehistoric settlement and field system. You may be able to pick out several hut circles which are over 2000 years old. The local community took the initiative in clearing access to this scheduled ancient monument. Retrace your steps to resume the Way along the minor road.

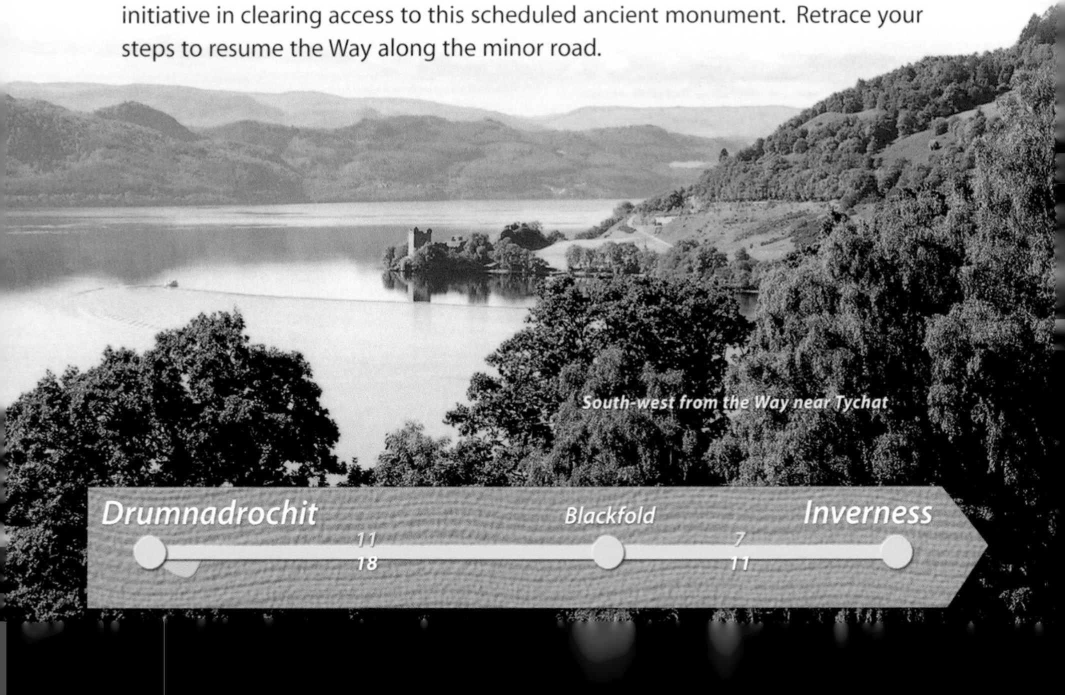

South-west from the Way near Tychat

You follow the road across the Abriachan plateau for over an hour, accompanied by fine views of the Glen Afffric and Strathfarrar hills to the north and west. Later comes your first glimpse of the Beauly Firth to the north-east. This meets the Moray Firth at Inverness, and is the first sign of your destination.

The road descends to Blackfold, where you bear left on to a track through Craig Leach forest, mainly populated by pine, but with wide paths and plenty of light and shade. Beneath you and out of sight, Loch Ness has given way to tiny Loch Dochfour and the River Ness.

You walk through mixed broadleaved forest, then leave the forest track to descend into the open ground above Craig Dunain, a vast building which used to be a mental hospital. Leachkin chambered cairn is nearby, but not visible from the Way. Look north for the hill on which Craig Phadrig stands: see page 22.

The Way follows a path down the hill, between houses, across a minor road, to General Booth Road. After an underpass it goes alongside the golf course, past a playing field, to meet the Caledonian Canal for the first time since Fort Augustus. (Refer to the plan on page 60, but note that its north is straight up, whereas north is rotated on the drop-down map.)

Cross the canal at Tomnahurich Bridge and turn right down Bught Road, past the Floral Hall (with coffee shop). At Whin Park turn left and follow the Way as it crosses the river by way of Ness Islands.

Once on the east bank, a path between river and road takes you past the Infirmary Footbridge, named after the Royal Northern Infirmary opposite, which now houses the headquarters of the University of the Highlands and Islands.

Within minutes you leave the riverside to cross the road at Ness Bank Church and turn left up View Place to reach your final destination, Inverness castle.

The Ness Islands Footbridge

3·7 The destination: Inverness

The site of Inverness has been inhabited for at least 7000 years, and is full of historic interest. Neolithic stone circles and passage-type burial cairns have been found in and near the town. In the nineteenth century, it benefited from the arrival of the railways and the building of the Caledonian Canal, and many of its fine public buildings are Victorian.

In 1982, there was a further boost to communications in the opening of the Kessock suspension bridge which takes the A9 trunk north across the Beauly Firth. With the expansion of Inverness Airport, it is nowadays well connected by road, rail, water and air. Always regarded as the 'capital of the Highlands', Inverness was awarded city status in 2001.

The terminus of the Great Glen Way is marked by a stone monument, the partner of the one at Fort William. It stands at Inverness Castle, which was built on the site of a much older royal castle. By 1718 it had a large tower house, bastioned by General Wade, and a court-house was added in 1843. Part of it was originally a prison but later it became a sheriff court. A Castle Garrison Encounter is staged daily except Sundays, from March to November (telephone 01463 243 363).

Nearby in Castle Wynd, there is a Tourist Information Centre and the museum and art gallery. The latter houses displays on the Great Glen, the Caledonian Canal and Highland heritage and folk life, including Jacobite tartans and other costumes. It is open daily except Sundays, year-round (telephone 01463 237 114).

Inverness Castle

St Andrew's Cathedral stands beside the River Ness, its twin towers a distinctive landmark. It was founded by Bishop Eden, but designed by the town's Provost, Alexander Ross. Work began in 1866 and within three years it had reached almost its present form. Ross had intended 200-foot spires to complete the towers, but they were abandoned because of rising costs.

Next to the cathedral is the Eden Court Theatre, a multi-purpose complex with an 800-seat theatre, a conference centre and an art gallery. The main theatre was closed for refurbishment in 2005/06. Telephone 01463 234 234 for an update and free guide to events year-round.

There are two side-trips that you can complete on foot, or assisted by public transport, either separately or combined. The first is to complete your 'coast-to-coast' journey by visiting Clachnaharry sea lock: see page 21. The second is to visit the vitrified fort of Craig Phadrig: see page 22.

If you haven't yet cruised on Loch Ness, you might consider a boat trip. The Jacobite Queen leaves from Tomnahurich Bridge, which the Way passes over in its approach to Inverness.

Further afield, you might wish to visit Culloden, the battlefield where the Jacobites were finally defeated in 1746. A ceremony is held every year on the Saturday closest to the anniversary (16 April). It's five miles to the east on the B9006, with a visitor centre open daily from February to December (telephone 01463 790 607). A mile further east lies the prehistoric remains at Clava Cairns, with two passage graves and a ring cairn (2500-2000 BC), also open year-round.

Inverness town plan

Reference

Contact details

All telephone numbers are shown as dialled from within the UK. To dial from another country, use the access code then 44 followed by the number below minus its leading zero. Numbers beginning 08 may work only within the UK. Contacts were checked before publication, but details are liable to change.

Accommodation & services

The free booklet *Accommodation & Services Guide* is updated annually and available from:

The Great Glen Way Rangers
Auchterawe
Fort Augustus
PH32 4BT
Phone/fax 01320 366 633

Details are also on their website:

www.greatglenway.com

Forestry Commission

The Forestry Commission is responsible for managing, protecting and expanding Britain's forests and woodlands. The relevant Forest Districts are Fort Augustus (01320 366322) and Lochaber (01397 702184). The free leaflets *Great Glen Forest Walks* and *Great Glen Mountain Bike Route* can be requested from the Inverness office (01463 232 811) or either of the above.

www.forestry.gov.uk

Scottish Natural Heritage and SOAC

Scottish Natural Heritage is Scotland's prinicipal nature conservation agency. Its website is

www.snh.org.uk and details of the Scottish Outdoor Access Code are at

www.outdooraccess-scotland.com.

Phone 01738 458 545 for a free copy of the Code.

Notes for novices

For those who lack experience in long-distance walking, we have prepared notes on choosing and using gear. Visit our website:

www.rucsacs.com and click *Notes for novices*. Alternatively, send a suitably stamped addressed envelope to the address at the foot of the back cover.

Tourist Information Centres

The official website of the Scottish Tourist Board is at

www.visitscotland.com and its dedicated *walkingwild* section offers various free resources, see

walking.visitscotland.com

The website **www.visithighlands.com** is well worth a visit. Use it to request their *Freedom of the Highlands* brochure and local visitor guides with maps and accommodation listings. Click the link for **Walking** for useful information on walking festivals and links to providers.

Three of the five TICs on or near the Way are open year-round to visitors (Fort William, Spean Bridge and Inverness). From October to Easter, Fort Augustus is closed and Drumnadrochit has restricted hours. All phone enquiries to Visitscotland: tel 0845 225 5121

Highland Council operates the Glen Nevis Visitor Centre: 01397 705 922

Weather information

The Met Office is the most authoritative source on weather in Britain, and operates the Weathercall service that provides forecasts by phone or fax. For West Highlands call 09014 722 075 and for East Highlands 09014 722 074 (premium rate charges). Visit their website:

www.metoffice.com

For hill-climbing, refer to the Mountain Weather Information Service website:

www.mwis.org.uk

Service providers

The Scottish Activity Holiday Association maintains a register of providers, see

www.activity-scotland.org.uk.

See also our Links page at

www.rucsacs.com/books/ggw/ for some recommended operators who offer booking and support services.

Caledonian Canal and boat charter

The Caledonian Canal Office is at Muirtown Wharf Inverness IV3 5LS tel 01463 233 140

The canal operates from 0800 to 1730 on weekdays, and in summer is open also at weekends; sea locks are tidal. Check their website for updates:

www.scottishcanals.co.uk

For boat charter, contact:
Caley Cruisers Ltd, Inverness
01463 236 328
website **www.caleycruisers.com**

Hostels

The Scottish Youth Hostels Association website gives details of hostels and accepts online bookings. Membership is optional, no upper age limit. Prices range from £7-£15 per night, sheet sleeping bag provided, tel
01786 891 400.
website **www.syha.org.uk**

Scottish Independent Hostels maintains a list of affiliated independent hostels, see website **www.hostel-scotland.co.uk**
It produces a useful free booklet *Blue Hostel Guide* for which you can send an sae or access its content online.

Travel and transport

Traveline
0870 608 2608 **www.traveline.org.uk**
Scottish Citylink (buses)
08705 505 050 **www.citylink.co.uk**
National train enguiries
08457 484 950 **www.the trainline.com**
bmi
0870 6070 555 **www.flybmi.com**
British Airways
0870 8509 850 **www.ba.com**
easyJet
0870 6000 000 **www.easyjet.com**
British Airports Authority
www.baa.co.uk

Glasgow Airport	0870 040 0008
Edinburgh Airport	0870 040 0007
Aberdeen Airport	0870 040 0006
Inverness Airport	01463 232 471

Other websites

A web search will reveal thousands of websites on the Great Glen, Loch Ness and local history. The Loch Ness 2000 Project maintains a good archive on the scientific explorations of Loch Ness:
www.loch-ness-scotland.com

The Royal Commission on Ancient and Historic Monuments maintains a database on interesting sites, including the Great Glen hill forts:
www.rcahms.gov.uk/canmore.html

Stockscotland (formerly the Scottish Highland Photo Library) website is at
www.stockscotland.com
(phone 01862 892 298).

Ben Nevis

If you plan to climb Ben Nevis, obtain the free 8-page Mountaineering Council of Scotland leaflet *Navigation on Ben Nevis*. It contains a map clip, aerial photograph and detailed advice and instructions. The content is also on their website
www.mountaineering-scotland.org.uk

Further reading

The books below are reasonably priced and recommended.

Cameron, A D (2005) *The Caledonian Canal* Birlinn ISBN 1-84158-403-7
New edition of a well-respected account of the canal's construction and recent history

McKirdy, A and Crofts, R (1999) *Scotland: the Creation of its Natural Landscape* Scottish Natural Heritage 64 pp ISBN 0-85397-004-2
Well-illustrated and readable account of how geology fashions landscapes

Sinclair, Charles (1998) *A Wee Guide to the Jacobites* Goblilnshead 88 pp ISBN 1-899874-14-3
Readable, concise and informative, with a list of places to visit and many b/w photographs

Tabraham, C *Urquhart Castle: the Official Souvenir Guide* Historic Scotland 48 pp ISBN 1-903570-30-1

Maps

Harvey's Map Services publishes a Great Glen Way route map (1:40,000) and a detailed map for Ben Nevis (1:25,000). The Ordnance Survey Landranger Series (1:50,000) covers the Great Glen in three sheets (26, 34 and 41).

Acknowledgements

The authors are very grateful to the following for help of various kinds, especially to those who commented on the manuscript in whole or in part: the Great Glen Way Rangers, the Highland Council's Great Glen Way Steering Group, Cattie Anderson (SNH), Jack MacKay (FC), Alastair MacLeod, Sir Robert Megarry, Adrian Shine, Malcolm Wield and Sandra Reid (Paul). Their efforts resulted in many improvements but of course we are responsible for any flaws that may remain.

We welcome comments from readers, preferably by email to **info@rucsacs.com**.

Photo credits

The publisher is grateful for permission from the following to reproduce their images: **Sandra Bardwell** p26, p31, p55; **Caley Cruisers** p20 (upper), **Clan Cameron Museum** p43; **Great Glen Way Rangers** p7, p9; **Forestry Commission** p34 (upper), p35 (both), p36 (upper); **Visitscotland** p14, p37, p41 lower, p44, p47 (upper), p48, p49, p50, p51, p57, p59; **Loch Ness 2000** p16; **A and P Macdonald** (front cover); **Jacquetta Megarry** title page, p4, p5, p8, p10 (both), p18, p19, p20 (lower), p21 (both), p24, p25, p28, p29, p36 (lower), p41 (upper), p46 (both), p47 (lower), p52, p53, p54, p58 (upper)/p60; **NERC Satellite Receiving Station**, University of Dundee p17; **Andrew Pointer** p38/back cover; **Colin Simpson** p22, p42, p45, p56, p58 lower; **www.stockscotland.com** p32 (both), p34 (lower), p37 (upper), p40; **www.rspb-images.com** p33 (lower).

Rucksack Readers

Rucksack Readers has published books covering long-distance walks in Scotland, Ireland and worldwide (the Alps, China, Peru and Tanzania). Its 2005 series *Rucksack Pocket Summits* is for climbers of the world's 'seven summits'. For more information, or to order online, visit **www.rucsacs.com**. To order by telephone, dial 01786 824 696 (outside UK dial +44 1786 824 696).

ISBN 1-898481-19-9

ISBN 1-898481-13-X

ISBN 1-898481-21-0

ISBN 1-898481-22-9

ISBN 1-898481-14-8

ISBN 1-898481-12-1

ISBN 1-898481-23-7

ISBN 1-898481-17-2

ISBN 1-898481-20-2

ISBN 1-898481-51-2

Index

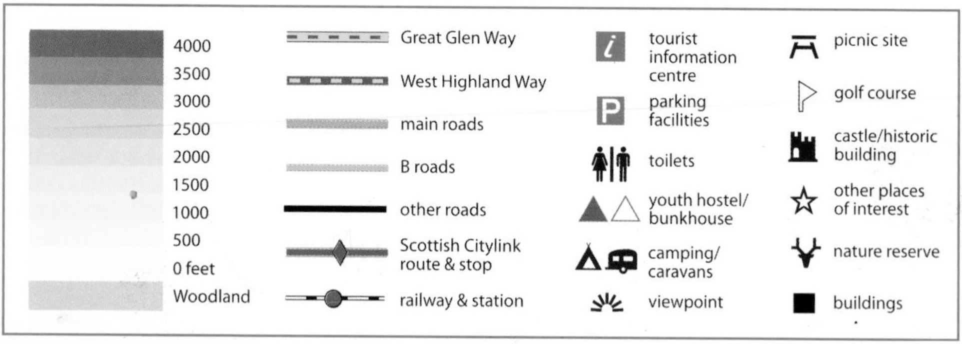

4000
3500
3000
2500
2000
1500
1000
500
0 feet
Woodland
Great Glen Way
West Highland Way
main roads
B roads
other roads
Scottish Citylink route & stop
railway & station
tourist information centre
parking facilities
toilets
youth hostel/ bunkhouse
camping/ caravans
viewpoint
picnic site
golf course
castle/historic building
other places of interest
nature reserve
buildings